ULTIMATE DRUM PLAY-ALONG

BOOK & PLAY-ALONG CDs
WITH TONE 'N' TEMPO CHANGER

LED ZEPPELIN

Play Along with 8 Great-

About the TNT Changer

Use the TNT software to change keys, loop playback, and mute tracks for play-along. For complete instructions, see the *TnT ReadMe.pdf* file on your enhanced CDs.

Windows users: insert a CD into your computer, double-click on My Computer, right-click on your CD drive icon, and select Explore to locate the file.

Mac users: insert a CD into your computer and double-click on the CD icon on your desktop to locate the file.

Alfred

Produced by
Alfred Music Publishing Co., Inc.
P.O. Box 10003
Van Nuys, CA 91410-0003
alfred.com

Printed in USA.

ISBN-10: 0-7390-5944-0 (Book & 2 CDs)
ISBN-13: 978-0-7390-5944-9 (Book & 2 CDs)

Cover photo: courtesy of Michael Putland / Retna

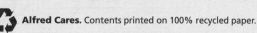
Alfred Cares. Contents printed on 100% recycled paper.

LED ZEPPELIN

Contents

Drum Charts*

* For your convenience, printable PDF versions of the drum charts are embedded on the enhanced CDs.

4

EDITOR'S NOTE

It is simply impossible to actually recreate the recorded performances of Led Zeppelin and the production techniques of Jimmy Page. The intention of these recordings is to aid in the study of the drum parts by providing credible tracks to play along with, hopefully capturing the spirit of the original music. Ultimately, it is essential to listen to, and try and emulate, the original Led Zeppelin tracks to really understand the musical nuance, intensity, and brilliance of those recordings.

CREDITS

Supervisory editors: Brad Tolinski and Jimmy Brown
Project manager and music editor: Tom Farncombe
Audio recording and mixing: Jonas Persson
Guitars and guitar transcriptions: Arthur Dick
Additional transcription and editing: Jimmy Brown
Bass guitar and bass transcriptions: Paul Townsend
Drums, percussion, and drum transcriptions: Noam Lederman
Keyboards and keyboard transcriptions: Paul Honey
Music engraving: Paul Ewers Music Design
Thanks to Chandler Guitars (www.chandlerguitars.co.uk).

Special thanks to Mark Lodge at Hiwatt UK for supplying the Hiwatt 100 Head, an exact replica of Jimmy Page's amp from the Led Zeppelin sessions. **HIWATT**
WWW.HIWATT.CO.UK

DRUM KEY

EQUIPMENT LIST

Drums

1968 Ludwig drum kit (24" bass drum, 13" rack tom, 16" floor tom, 18" second floor tom)

Ludwig 6.5 x 14" Supraphonic snare drum, Ludwig 8 x 14" Coliseum snare drum

Paiste cymbals

Guitars

1952 Goldtop Gibson Les Paul reissue

1959 Gibson Les Paul

1969 Fender Telecaster

1969 Black Beauty Gibson Les Paul

1972 Fender Telecaster

Guitar Effects

Celmo Sardine Can compressor

Pete Cornish sustain pedal

Jim Dunlop Crybaby wah-wah pedal

Eventide flanger

Fulltone Full-Drive 2

Lexicon PCM91

Line 6 MM4 modulation pedal

Manley valve EQ

Roger Mayer Treble Booster

Roger Mayer Voodoo Vibe + vibrato unit

Tube-Tech CL 1B valve compressor

Universal Audio DI

Violin bow

Guitar Amplifiers

Cornell Romany 10 watt

Hiwatt 100

Marshall JCM2000

1965 VOX AC30

1964 Watkins Electronics Westminster 5 watt combo

Bass

1991 Fender Jazz Bass

1978 Fender Precision Bass

1962 reissue Fender Jazz Bass (strung with flatwound strings and used to emulate John Paul Jones's organ pedal performance on "Since I've Been Loving You")

Ashdown bass amplification

Miscellaneous

Nord Electro 2 modelling keyboard

Studer A80 tape machine

BLACK DOG

Words and Music by
JIMMY PAGE, ROBERT PLANT
and JOHN PAUL JONES

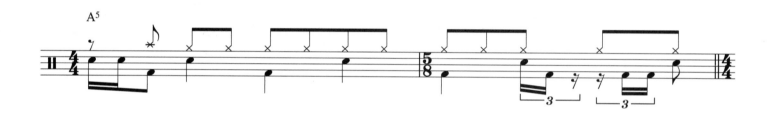

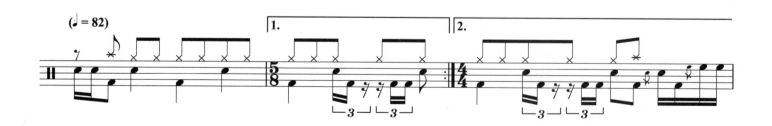

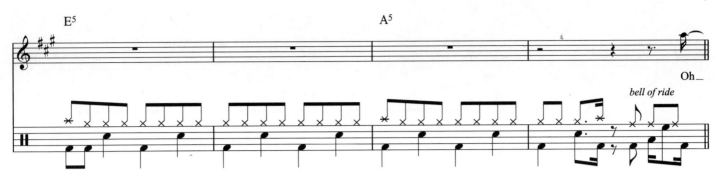

Oh __

__ yeah, oh __ yeah, oh, __ oh, __ oh. __ Oh __

__ yeah, __ oh, __ yeah, __ oh, __ oh, __ oh. __ 4. Well

Freely

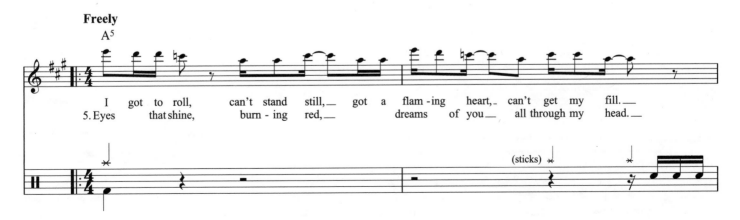

I got to roll, can't stand still, __ got a flam-ing heart, can't get my fill. __
5. Eyes that shine, burn-ing red, __ dreams of you __ all through my head. __

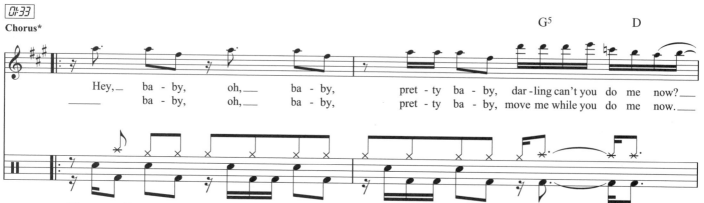

*The metre of this song is somewhat controversial, especially in the **Chorus** and **Solo** sections.
Previous editions suggest that the kick drum indicates the downbeat, meaning irregular bars at certain points.
However, the drum clicks and cues before these sections would make it seem that the metre actually remains constant, in 4/4;
therefore the snare drum remains on the backbeat throughout. This is reflected in this arrangement.

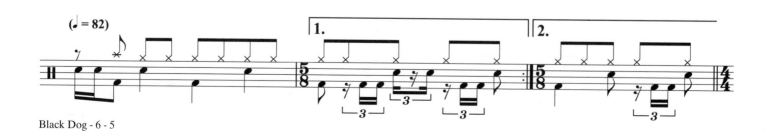

Ah ah, ah ah, ah ah, ah ah, ah ah, ah ah,

03:23
Outro Solo

Repeat ad lib. to fade

Black Dog - 6 - 6

COMMUNICATION BREAKDOWN

Words and Music by
JIMMY PAGE, JOHN PAUL JONES and JOHN BONHAM

Communication Breakdown - 4 - 1

you let me hold you, let me feel your lov-ing touch?
I'm nev-er gon-na let you go 'cause I like your charms.

00:35

Chorus

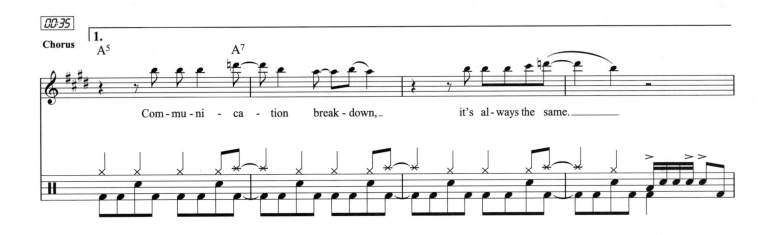

Com-mu-ni - ca - tion break-down, it's al-ways the same.

Hav-ing a ner - vous break-down, drive me in-sane.

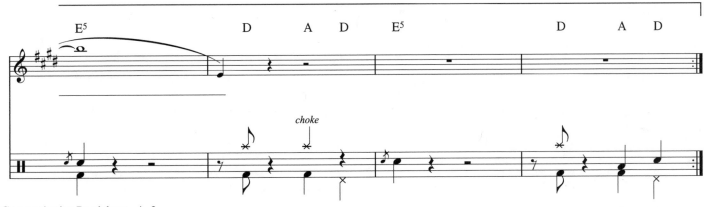

choke

Communication Breakdown - 4 - 2

Communication Breakdown - 4 - 3

DAZED AND CONFUSED

Words and Music by
JIMMY PAGE

and a-buse___ tell-ing all of your lies,___ run 'round sweet ba-by, Lord, how you hyp-no-tise.

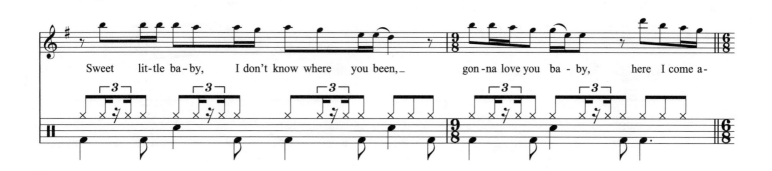

Sweet lit-tle ba-by, I don't know where you been,___ gon-na love you ba-by, here I come a-

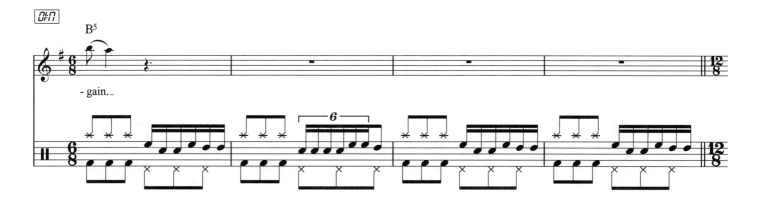

B⁵

-gain.

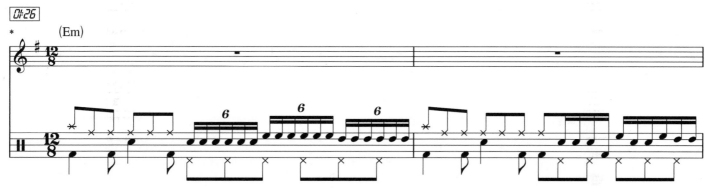

(Em)

* *The original versions of this song by Jake Holmes, and by Jimmy Page with the Yardbirds, clearly place the low E of the signature bass line riff on beat 1 and the high G on beat 2. In the first 2 verses John Bonham chooses to turn the metre around, placing the high G on beat 1. From this point on he clearly turns the metre around again, placing the high G on beat 2 as in the original versions. He remains in this metre for the rest of the song. All subsequent versions of this song follow this exact same pattern of turning the metre around.*

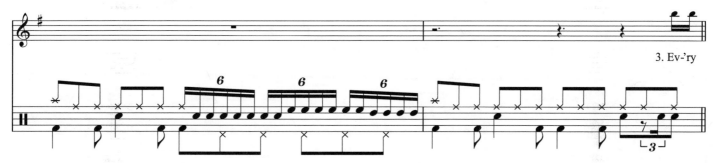

3. Ev-'ry

Dazed and Confused - 8 - 2

Interlude

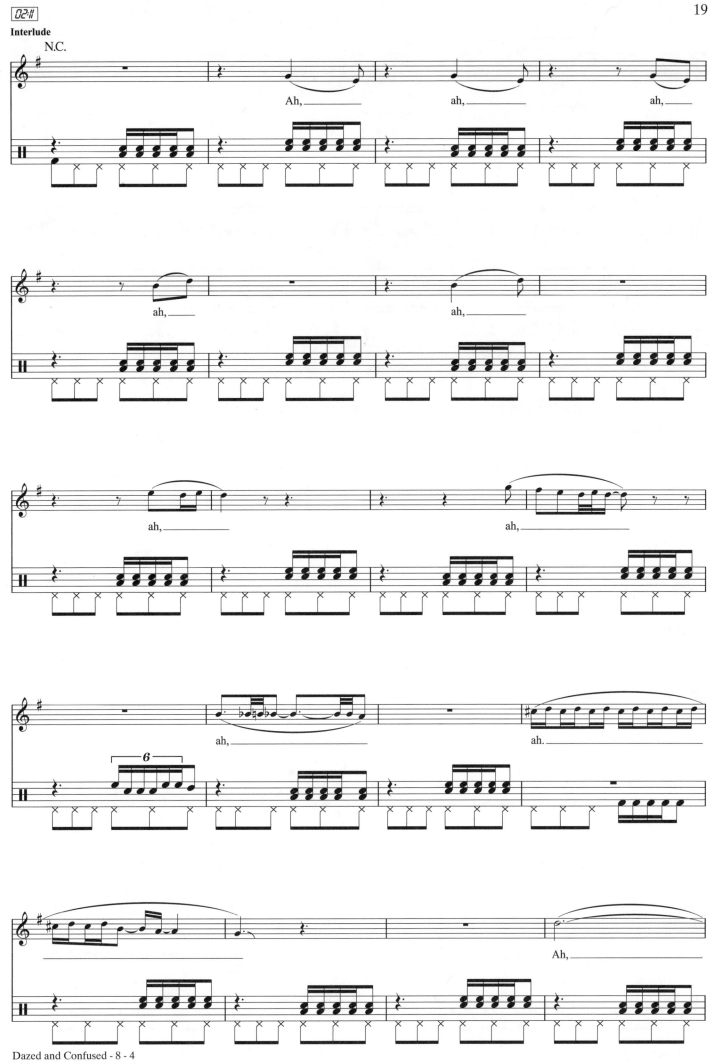

Dazed and Confused - 8 - 6

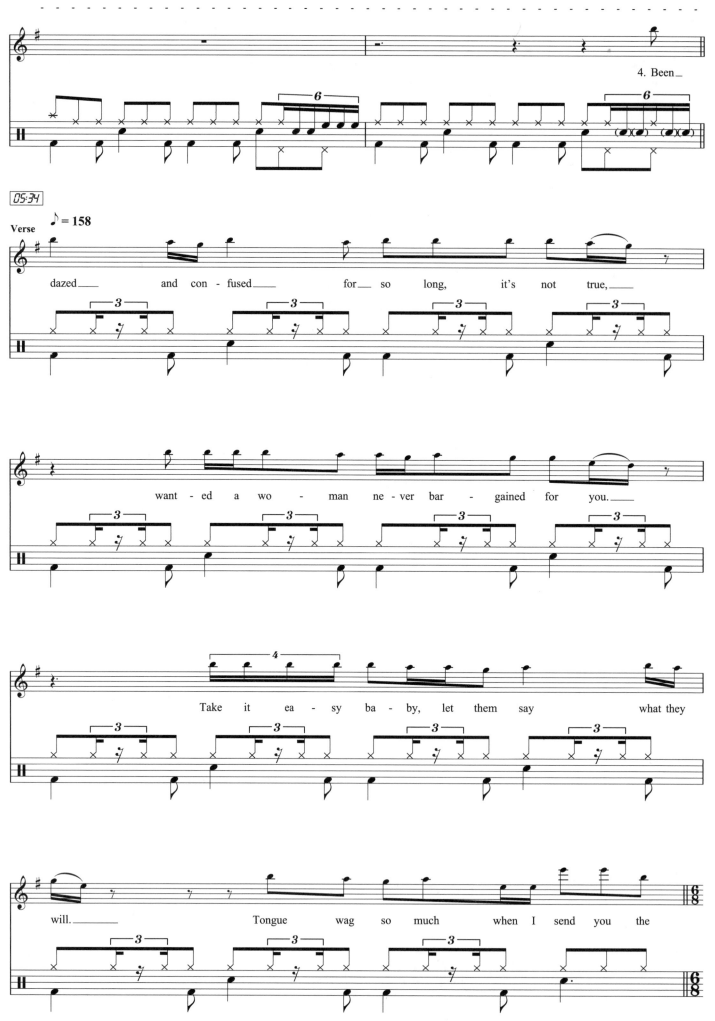

4. Been

05:34

Verse ♪ = 158

dazed____ and con - fused____ for__ so long, it's not true,____

want - ed a wo - man ne - ver bar - gained for you.____

Take it ea - sy ba - by, let them say what they

will.____ Tongue wag so much when I send you the

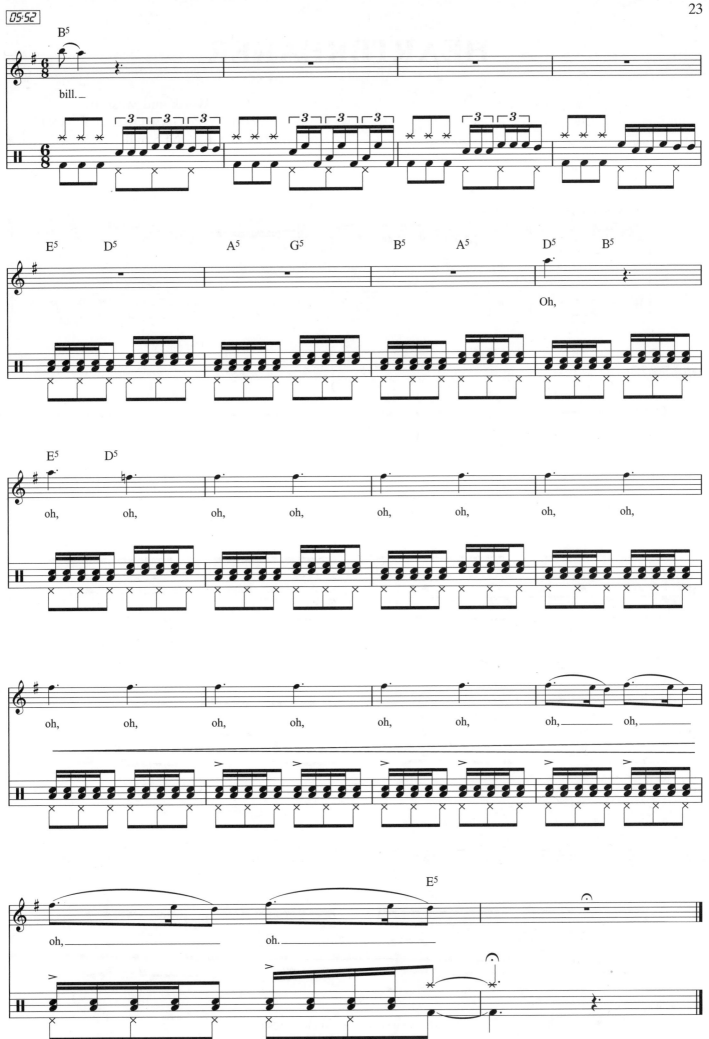

HEARTBREAKER

Words and Music by
JIMMY PAGE, ROBERT PLANT,
JOHN PAUL JONES and JOHN BONHAM

Heartbreaker - 5 - 1

IMMIGRANT SONG

Words and Music by
JIMMY PAGE and ROBERT PLANT

Immigrant Song - 3 - 1

Immigrant Song - 3 - 3

ROCK AND ROLL

Words and Music by
JIMMY PAGE, ROBERT PLANT,
JOHN PAUL JONES and JOHN BONHAM

been a long time since I rock and rolled.

(2.) been a long time since the book of love.

1. It's

It's

(I)

been a long time since I did the stroll._____ Ooh,
can't count the tears of a life___ with no love._____

(D⁵)

let me get it back, let me get (it) back, let me get back,___ ba-by, where I___ come from.
Car-ry me back, car-ry me back, car-ry me back,___ ba-by, where I___ come from.

*crash 1° only

(A⁵)

_____ Oh,___ oh. It's

*crash 1° only

1.
(E⁵)   (D⁵)

been a long time, been a long time, been a long, lone-ly, lone-ly, lone-ly, lone-ly, lone-ly

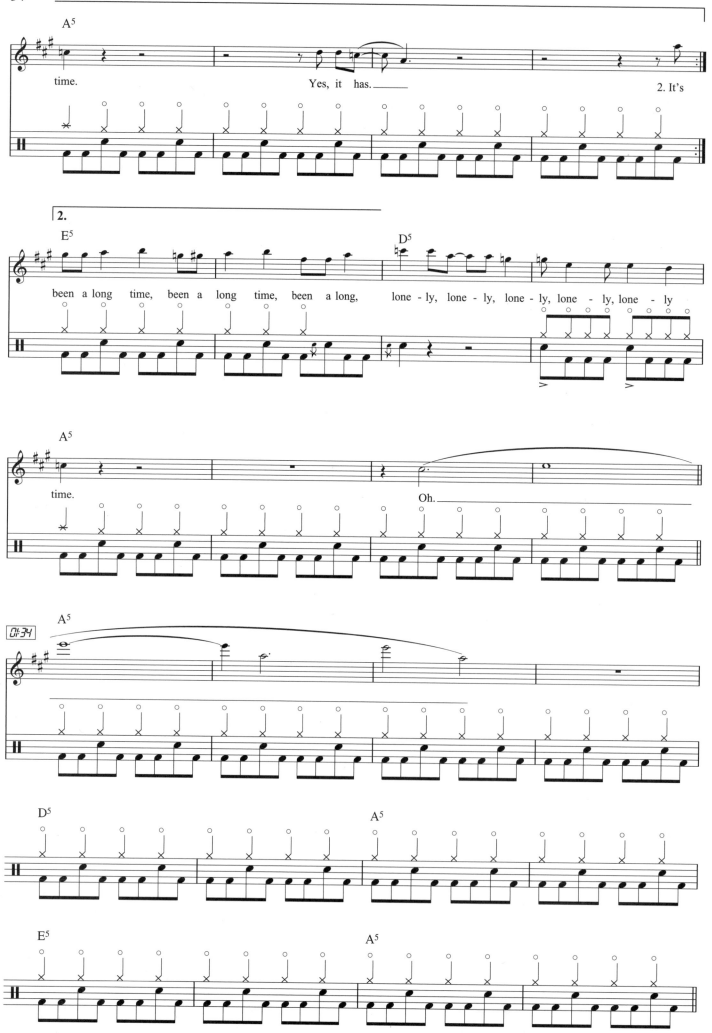

Rock and Roll - 6 - 4

Rock and Roll - 6 - 6

SINCE I'VE BEEN LOVING YOU

Words and Music by
JIMMY PAGE, ROBERT PLANT
and JOHN PAUL JONES

Since I've Been Loving You - 8 - 1

Since I've Been Loving You - 8 - 2

Since I've Been Loving You - 8 - 4

44

Since I've Been Loving You - 8 - 8

WHOLE LOTTA LOVE

Words and Music by
JIMMY PAGE, ROBERT PLANT, JOHN PAUL JONES,
JOHN BONHAM and WILLIE DIXON

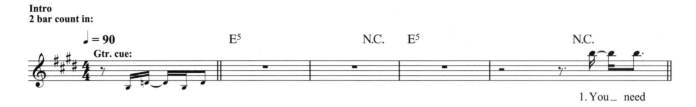

Whole Lotta Love - 6 - 1

Shake_ for me, girl.

I wan - na be your back - door man...

(vocal continues ad lib.)

repeat ad lib. to fade

Drum Charts

BLACK DOG

Words and Music by
JIMMY PAGE, ROBERT PLANT
and JOHN PAUL JONES

Black Dog - 2 - 1

COMMUNICATION BREAKDOWN

Words and Music by
JIMMY PAGE, JOHN PAUL JONES and JOHN BONHAM

Communication Breakdown - 2 - 1

Chorus

Communication Breakdown - 2 - 2

DAZED AND CONFUSED

Words and Music by
JIMMY PAGE

Dazed and Confused - 4 - 1

Verse

Interlude

HEARTBREAKER

Words and Music by
JIMMY PAGE, ROBERT PLANT,
JOHN PAUL JONES and JOHN BONHAM

Intro
1 bar count in:
♩ = 94

Verse

Bridge

Heartbreaker - 3 - 1

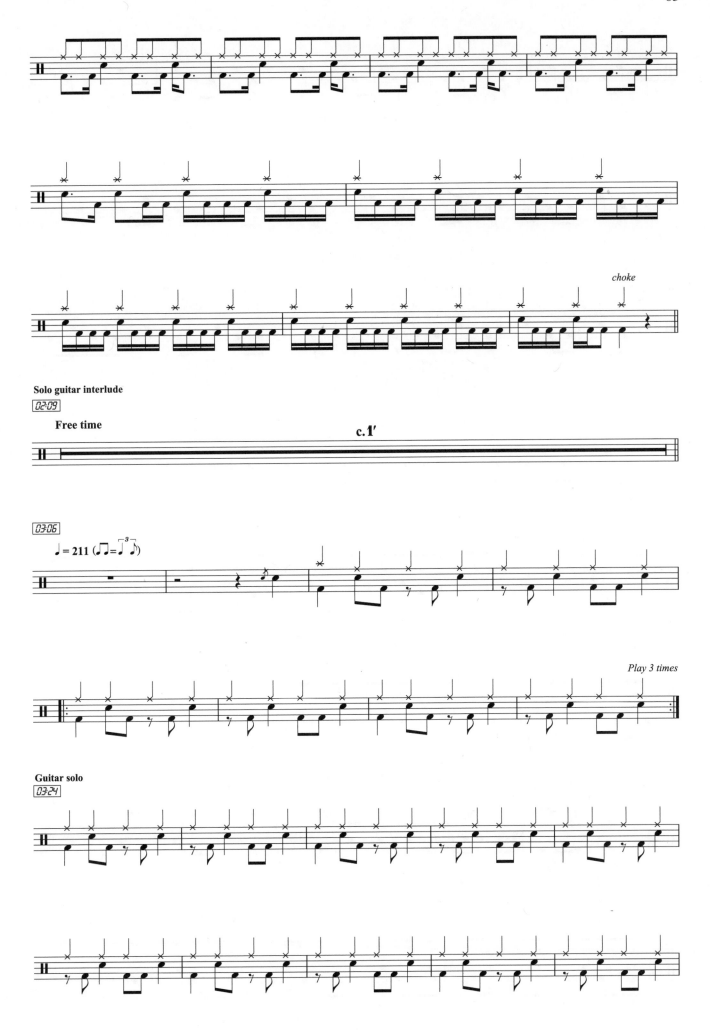

Solo guitar interlude

Free time

c. 1'

Guitar solo

64

Heartbreaker - 3 - 3

IMMIGRANT SONG

Words and Music by
JIMMY PAGE and ROBERT PLANT

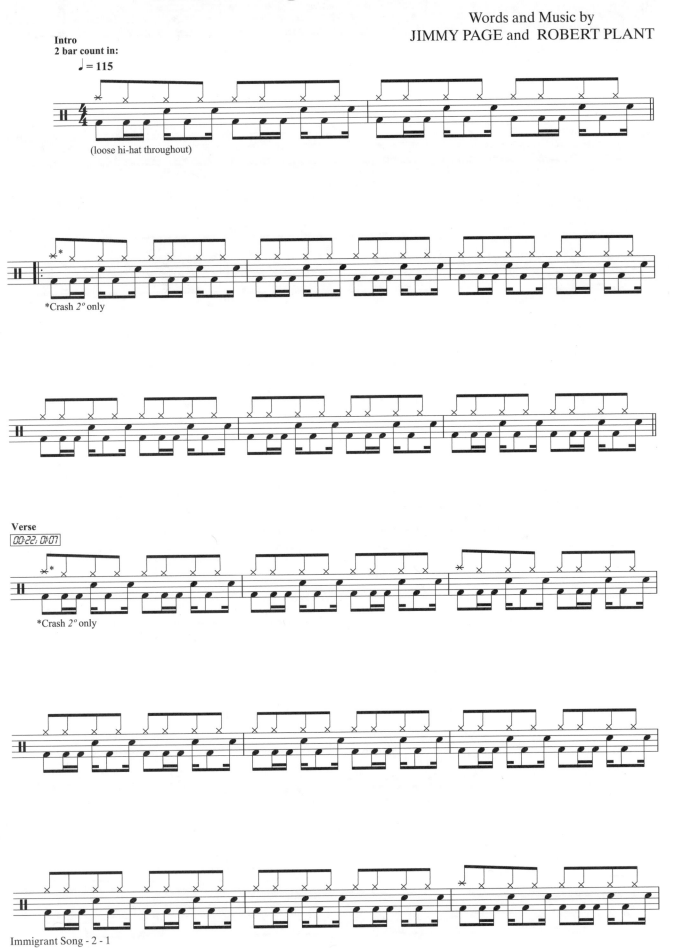

Immigrant Song - 2 - 1

66

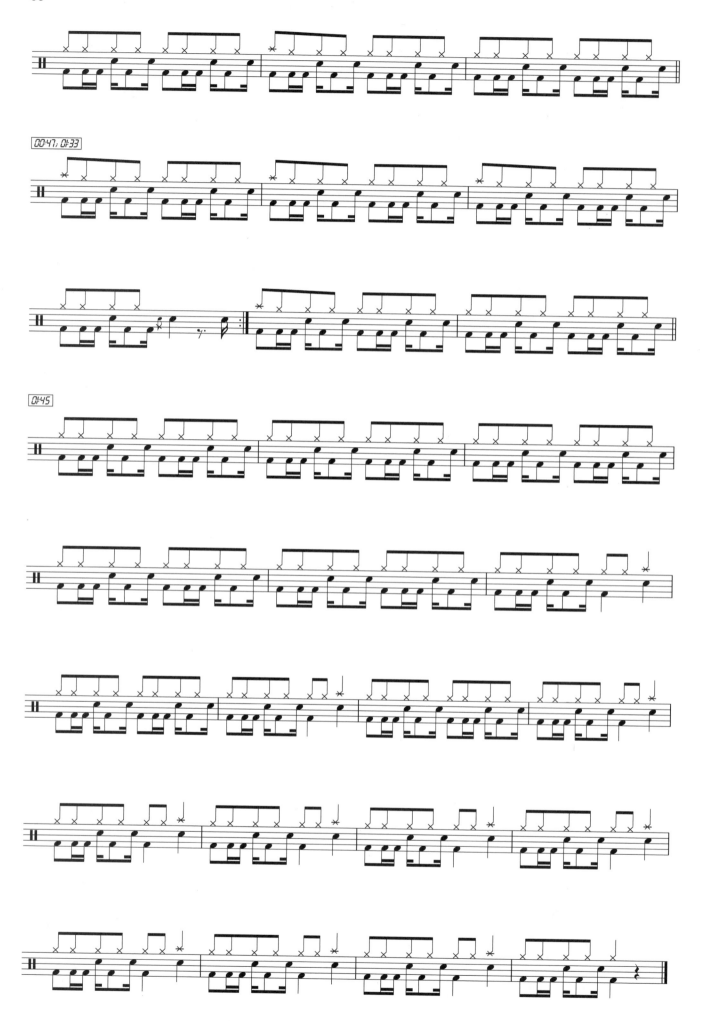

ROCK AND ROLL

Words and Music by
JIMMY PAGE, ROBERT PLANT,
JOHN PAUL JONES and JOHN BONHAM

Rock and Roll - 4 - 1

68

Verse
`0:00`

`0:34`

Guitar solo
`0:50`

Verse
02:24

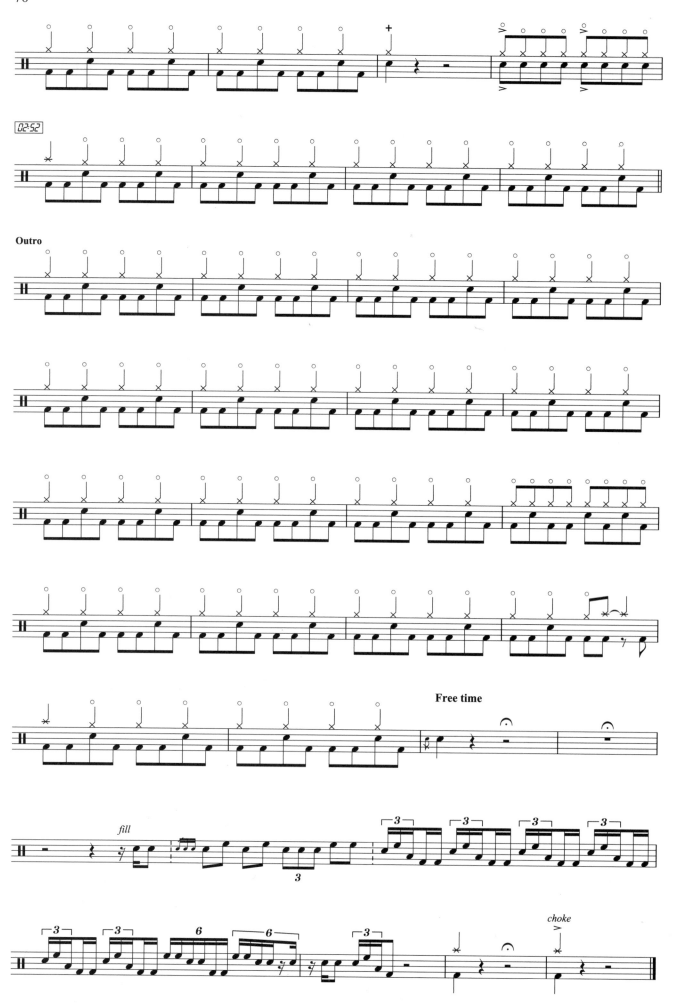

SINCE I'VE BEEN LOVING YOU

Words and Music by
JIMMY PAGE, ROBERT PLANT
and JOHN PAUL JONES

Since I've Been Loving You - 4 - 1

Verse
02:29

Guitar solo
03:39

Since I've Been Loving You - 4 - 3

Since I've Been Loving You - 4 - 4

WHOLE LOTTA LOVE

Words and Music by
JIMMY PAGE, ROBERT PLANT, JOHN PAUL JONES,
JOHN BONHAM and WILLIE DIXON

Keep HH foot 8's and improvise cymbal bell part

Whole Lotta Love - 3 - 1

Guitar solo

Verse

Chorus

Freely

Outro

04:23

Repeat ad lib. to fade

Alfred